Fantastic Kids

Theater Kids

Dona Herweck Rice

Publishing Credits

Rachelle Cracchiolo, M.S.Ed., *Publisher*
Conni Medina, M.A.Ed., *Managing Editor*
Nika Fabienke, Ed.D., *Series Developer*
June Kikuchi, *Content Director*
John Leach, *Assistant Editor*
Kevin Pham, *Graphic Designer*

Image Credits: p.8: Bettmann / Getty Images; p.9: Daniel Zuchnik/FilmMagic/Getty Images; p.10: Photofest; p.11: Bill Ray/The LIFE Picture Collection/Getty Images; p.12: Boston Globe / Getty Images; pp.14, 15: Joan Marcus/Photofest © Walt Disney Productions; pp.16, 17: Michael Dodge/Getty Images; pp.18,19: John Phillips/Getty Images; pp.20, 21: Bettmann / Contributor / Getty Images; pp.22, 23: David M. Benett/Getty Images; all other images from iStock and/or Shutterstock.

Teacher Created Materials
5301 Oceanus Drive
Huntington Beach, CA 92649-1030
http://www.tcmpub.com

ISBN 978-1- 4258-4960-3

Printed by: VIN#973
Printed In: China
PO11140

Table of Contents

Bravo!

There is no business like show business, and these kids know it. They are **theater** kids. They sing, dance, and act on stage.

Audiences love what theater kids do. They show their love with thunderous **applause**. Bravo!

Theater kids work hard. They train every day. They also must go to school.

Most of all, they must work well with others.
It takes many people to put on a show!

Andrea McArdle

Kids to Know

The play *Annie* is often on stage.
Andrea McArdle was the first girl to play Annie.
Annie is the star of the show.

Other kids are in the play, too. They play orphans. They sing and act together.

Daisy Eagan

Daisy Eagan starred in *The Secret Garden*.
She played Mary.
She won an award called the Tony.
She was just 11 years old.

Frankie Michaels starred in
Mame (MAYM).
He played Patrick.
He won a Tony Award, too!
He was also 11 years old.

Jojo is a lead role in *Seussical*.
The play is about the stories of Dr. Seuss.

Jojo is a Who in the play.
He helps save all the Whos.
Boys and girls have played
Jojo.

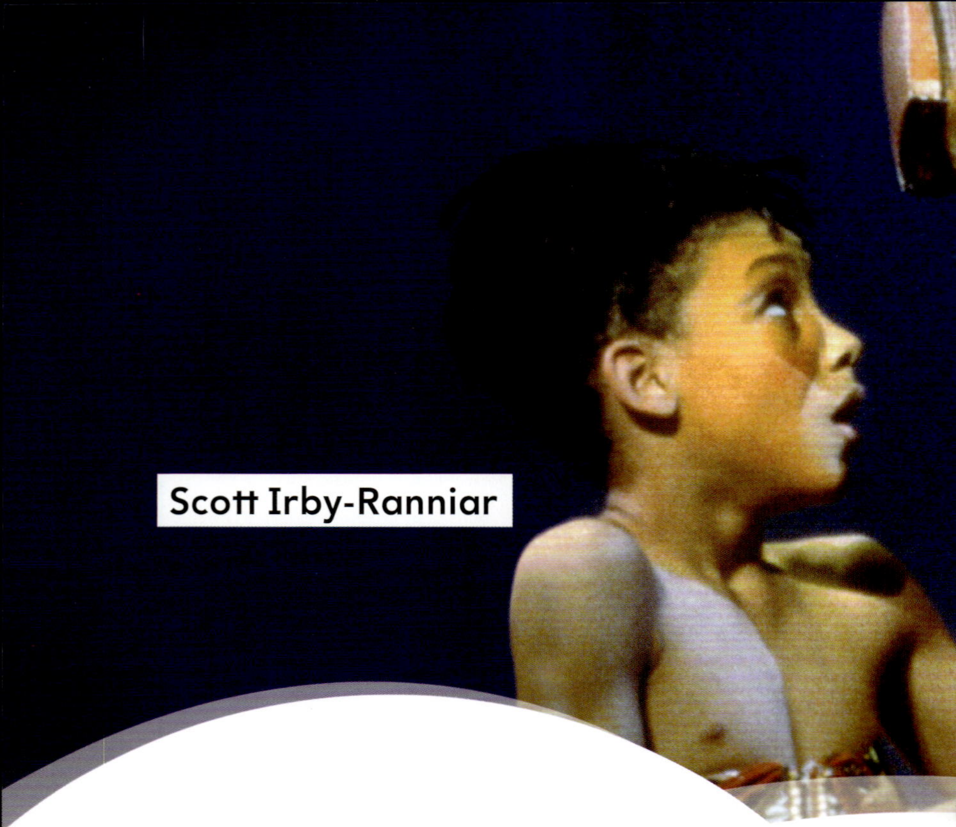

Scott Irby-Ranniar

In *The Lion King*, people play the roles. **Designers** help them look like animals. So do makeup artists.

Scott Irby-Ranniar was the first Young Simba.
He made the lion cub seem like a little boy.

Matilda is about a little girl.
She is very smart. But her parents treat her badly.
Three girls share the lead role.

Other kids are also in the show.
They play kids at school.
Matilda helps them and their teacher.

Many kids star in the musical *School of Rock*. The kids have to act, sing, and dance. They also have to play instruments!

In the play, the kids form a school rock band.
The actors really play music together on stage!

Not Kids

Some adults play kids in plays.
A woman plays Peter Pan.
But the character is a boy.

Adults are the kids in a show about Charlie Brown. Hair and makeup artists help them look young.

Fantastic Kids

It is not easy to be a kid in a play, but these theater kids make it work. They have talent, and they work hard.

They work with others to
make great shows.
They are fantastic kids!

Glossary

applause

designers

instruments

theater